NEW CALIFORNIA POETRY

Edited by	Robert Haas
	Calvin Bedient
	Brenda Hillman

The publisher gratefully acknowledges the generous contribution to this book provided by Joan Palevsky.

why

why not

why not

martha ronk

UNIVERSITY OF CALIFORNIA PRESS
Berkeley   Los Angeles   London

University of California Press

Berkeley and Los Angeles, California

University of California Press, Ltd.

London, England

For acknowledgments, please see page 85.

Library of Congress Cataloging-in-Publication Data

Ronk, Martha Clare.

   Why/why not / Martha Ronk.

      p.   cm.—(New California Poetry ; 8)

  ISBN 0-520-23623-8 (alk. paper)—

  ISBN 0-520-23811-7 (pbk. : alk. paper)

    I. Title. II. Series.

PS3568.O574 W48 2003

811'.54—dc21   2002035356

                                    CIP

Manufactured in Canada

12 11 10 09 08 07 06 05 04 03
10 9 8 7 6 5 4 3 2 1

The paper used in this publication meets the minimum
requirements of American National Standard for Information
Sciences—Permanence of Paper for Printed Library Materials,
ANSI-Z39.48-1984. ♾

for Dale

contents

- act 3 -

3 why/why not

- why -

- why not -

1 perplexities

In the perplexities

In the time it takes to fall asleep in unfamiliar surroundings
and given again the presence of a stranger in our midst
which of course oughtn't to unsettle the arrangements of anything
more or less nailed down or heavy enough to shove against the door
in case of incursions and alterations in the perplexities
of why he isn't speaking to me or if he had mailed it off
as he turned his back on the one who was walking by
baffled that in the space of a minute and given the open fields
there might be anyone in her narrow range of vision at all.

Each had been reading the night before

This explanation supersedes the prior only by reason of
its coming on the next page.
Each telltale image conceives of it differently from what
I might have said yesterday.
He took her head and forced it to the side and pushed at her hair.
And all this was done in the early morning to explain
the sounds out-of-doors and the book open on the table
from which each had been reading the night before.

In consequence

I am sitting with my feet to the side and therefore.
I am wearing a tan jacket and in consequence.
What follows is entirely dependent on.
The room positioned a replete and fully aligned body.
A chair made me and also sitting with a view.
One wishes to leap up and claim happiness or some such.
A composed demeanor then and for some moments to come.

Causality

From the events around the table even your mother was alive
    at the time
when she asked if I would come
and must therefore take some of the blame
having sat in the chair which is still there
which along with the measurements necessarily shifts the room.

Out there it's raining. The trees are on this side of
the Styx and we thank them for it. Well, we were looking for
the conjunction of the past and the present
but were willing to put up with a bit of each
watching the rain on one long afternoon.

A rational explanation

It might have been his usual demeanor.
All the lilies in yellow.
And the palpitations of his heart and weariness of tone
despite the ever-increasing light.
Some things weren't transported nor was he.
Although it might have been his usual demeanor
it was as unfamiliar given the circumstances
as to how they got between this side and that,
a rational explanation lurking all the while.
While on the contrary and in his left hand
all hope for an apparition as out of date as the Chinese chair
situated midway between the yellow ones and that other.

The placement of things

Your feet on the same steps
typing it in allegorical moments.
I'd like to think so. Also one's feet on the driveway.
What I said was I like tying my shoes
and he said children don't do it anymore.
Conceptually dense and enhanced by various means
nevertheless they balance and point.
When what I was thinking had nothing to do with
running into the wall which had suddenly thrown itself
across the room when I noticed the whereabouts of my hands
and the placement of paving stones with moss growing between them.

After the dark came

After the accident on the bricks we notice the undersides,
the light on the green stripes of the canna and our beating outside
    the house.
After the accident there were words between us and the stripes of
    the bamboo
hung like thunder we couldn't take our eyes off of.
After the plates fell and broke we stood in the way we stand
on one foot and turned our faces sideways.
I saw the stripes of veins in your forehead and moved
my own arms to my sides. After the dark came we came inside again.

Odi et amo, quare id faciam fortasse requiris?
nescio sed fieri sentio et excrucior.

CATULLUS, POEM 85

Odi et amo 1

Why is the cure for irony in loss I don't mind
losing but again you stand over there.
The one watching is the third and entirely unnecessary
party to the quiet whispering she came down the hills in.
Before long they'll leave together she'll
return to where she's from, I'll forget.
Someone else's forehead and shoulder is yesterday
is whispering don't mind me I haven't come.
Odd man out is the name and the stance
we assume entirely of our own accord.

Odi et amo 2

Do you think so. In the same house.
What makes you think so.
No one else I know.
The man with the mistaken hair
has been remembering what I remember but he thinks
are intrusive except ones I can't stand.
When my husband is writing a book,
when the children are waiting to be let in.
If it is this century I'm misplaced.
If the nineteenth, illumination shines.
The one I just saw likes measuring in increments
unmaking his bed and driving to Watertown.

Odi et amo 3

I'd like to, this century, murmur without end.
Or beginning to know where or even in the vicinity of.
Liking not to be diffuse, refused.
A system of nodes located in skin.
Now it is tied up, now it gets to me
lying at the door waiting for return.
Naturally environments count.
Naturally the formulation of degrees.
More of it throughout the day until it refers
to a completely different thing no matter what's
soaked through and through, no matter it's as prevalent.

Odi et amo 4

Allegory is the only way to conclusion.
Dubious with the growing grass I miss you.
You turned out to be long past the event.
Each geranium lent itself to the morning.
The amount of time spent counting.
Lifted out of herself and over the fence.
Several birds and several more birds.
Some things are quiet and others resolved.
When you became what I couldn't stop thinking.

2 why knowing is

why knowing is

And thus the native hue of resolution
Is sicklied o'er with the pale cast of thought,

Hamlet (3.1.84–85)

Why knowing is
(& Matisse's *Woman with a Hat*)

Why knowing is a quality out of fashion and no one can decide to
but slips into it or ends up with a painting one has never
seen that quality of light before even before having seen it
in between pages of another book and not remembering who knows
or recognizing the questionable quality of light on her face
as she sits for a portrait and isn't allowed to move an inch
you recognize the red silk flower on her hat
and can almost place where you have seen that gray descending
through the light reversing foreground and background
as the directions escape one as the way you have to
live with anyone as she gets up finally from her chair
having written the whole of it in her head as the question
ignored for the hundredth time as a quality of knowing is
oddly resuscitated from a decade prior to this.

How often, meaning what sort of quandariness

How often, meaning what sort of quandariness descends
like a cloud though not a cloud and not so easily defined—
even those who have walked to the edge of the sand
where it seems to begin, not even those can get it
the impossible sense of fog barely rift
wedged apart only by a line or two
the lower half lifted and lost at the horizon
as one is at not knowing one's response to another
who has come to be familiar as only the stranger who passes
again on the beach just to the left as if,
as lovers say, *I seem to have met you before or in another life,*
as a face emerging from the fog and walking directly into the camera
and smiling over the shoulder where you stand.

The decisions are already past

The decisions are already past the time in which
they were a folded crease or an envelope slipped
under the door or anywhere we walk the streets as before
but the tone's slipped a register more or less
on a vibrating string varying in length or perhaps it's
the moisture in the air or the flights of birds overhead

(was it lovely as walking is lovely)

as the gulls hovered before coming down to take food from
    her hand
she threw into the air, the air came down
to sail the paper airplane into the room where
distance becomes the point past which decisions are
no longer made or to-be-made but thresholds
across which they shift, bell-like, forward and back.

And so geography

And so geography puts one to sleep.
I couldn't tell how to get there
but thought to edit later
when I'd have a better sense of where it was,
even her account of the punky bricks
or of moss sidling up the side of tile
even standing in someone else's shoes
and wanting to fall asleep at the wheel
never remembering route numbers
or the lines of longitude and latitude
under the influence of omens like north or south
or how a person you knew years ago shows up by chance.

Hopelessly lost
(& a beach painting by Renoir)

Hopelessly lost in rooms under canopies striped green and white
blowing in the air and bright as flags over the boulevard
and flapping the sails of boats with irregular brushstrokes
across the bow she leans her face into the wind
finding something in the return whipped around the coast
which would have been slightly later in the century
although related as the bit of color in the margin repeats the red
on the straw hat as she circles around to the same place
to find what by then was a story of what would vanish in time
and the place uncertain as the awning scrolled up and down
in alternate patterns of light and shade over her face
and over tables arranged in plain view of the window overhead.

It seems the energy

It seems the energy would be better used
to dissipate tension in the room you happen to have taken
an apartment on the edge of town or some other walk
is closer to the park and she seems to like it
but whether or not it was a decision *per se*
is monumentally unclear as *stele, style, superimposition*
or the lassitude of Tuesday demands
no ultimate choice or even much looking back
to the curve of her profile everyone gets hooked on
the unseen other side but what seems clear is that all's
already in place, the variations no longer able to alter
the course of history but only to be contemplated
as the beauty of a statue is her face in a mirror.

If it is someone else's rent
(& van Gogh's *The Bedroom*)

If it is someone else's rent that must be walked to
and the signs are in Korean and you love someone
and you've already paid and the fears you have are
those of a witness porous enough but still at the periphery
and if you have to go so far all your muscles ache
the next day and the day after you have anticipated a certain pace
you know as well as the back of your hand
and the night is the waking blank and etched-over paper
of half-remembered ruinations you love as much as
you know how to love anything: *her face and refusal*
even when I point out we had the yellow bed for years
in spite of the printer's having botched the color
it anchored a queasiness of falling as they say to sleep
you could say with relief *like that* and point to
a picture above us hanging only slightly askew.

Unable to keep the spill from spilling

Unable to keep the spill from spilling over from concentration
to concentration the way a voice merges with a voice on tv
and *I shouldn't have left the house never have left the house*
weeks afterwards the fallout the spinout the stopped dead
in your tracks without cause without a car on the road
and if you slow down to watch the way one hour turns into
the next a rush of *I should never have left* gathered
in the spill of light from a window in a darkened room
or street lamps punching out squares in the plazas
across which shadows travel in and out
and the distance a warp into which oblong moments
torn from another year incise first one step and then the other.

Trying to move out

According to Jean-Luc Godard, the history of cinema is
boys photographing girls. The history of history, he said,
is boys burning girls at the stake.

Trying to move out of what's already established
as what it's called and as it fits into patterns recognizable
by anyone's point of view and trying not simply to shrug.

The way out is clear which is why so many cram at the shore
and stand under shoulder-draped towels
staring at the unending movement of waves

or listening for sounds echoing overhead
from the unearthly to the rhapsodic *there she is*
stepping on to the corner of a wooden stair to release a note

higher and thinner than the one before
or mesmerized before the mirror cutting off all one's hair
which is why Jean Seberg perhaps and the androgynous array

of recent incarnations seem not like clones or boys
but more to the point why she was picked to play the saint
and why they kept the fire burning as the cameras rolled.

The cause for wandering

The cause for wandering through the fading light
as occluded as one voice hidden from another
as the characters who make believe
by describing all events as possible *as if* events
always in the dark of night and in one scenario
conversing long distance with places as foreign as Slovenia
where in the backwoods of Eastern Europe
one tries to hunt up her former lover who doesn't recall
ever having heard her name.

In the church with angel heads
(& a portrait of Mary and child)

In the church with angel heads on chandeliers
hallucination draws a fiery wand as the closet opens
and without tremor lays bare the cross of stick on stick
and then it's gone or it's an accident that the subject returns
again when we're all seated or one recognizes only the background
coming forward as knees or subsiding into landscape
in the distance behind the head of one who sits forward,
her lap tipping the infant over the marble floor
who despite the laws of gravity doesn't fall
creating a miracle seated in an Umbrian town.

Waking from exhaustion

Waking from exhaustion and wrapping books in brown paper
and carting them to the post office and all the while talking rapid fire
without cessation to someone who is the final repository
of all that happened and takes notes in fine script
on the course of many years' sleeping and waking
and underlines important phrases still in the making
so that read back the following night under cover of darkness
one comes to understand as one keeps after a particular memory
lost in a drawer full of photos and note cards,
keeping pace with the wear and tear of accumulations
or counting how many need to be moved as touching the surfaces
in ritualized order or whose face won't ever come clear.

And yet

And yet what does *gets to me* mean
as that address to oneself
while wiping the mirror clean or scuffing the floor
seemingly unattached to the limb extended out across the linoleum
and how much time before it has weight
as losing one's watch yet again or watching the light
lengthen across the surface it could be hours before it
reaches the hallway or it could be hours earlier
given the restless twist of limbs who knows what bent of mind
as light in a pool of water angles off.

The very insignificance was what

The very insignificance was what pained the most
that so seemingly small a shudder as wind passing over
and leaving it exactly as it had been moments before
was what the slight had been, as easy and recurrent
as a dismissive wrist or a sighing shift
so that having spent the morning trying to get through
would make no difference, was so small a slight
as the passing of some capacity for marking a difference,
the wearing away of something so imperceptible
it wasn't until years had passed anyone could detect
that water, having found the path of least resistance,
had worn away some infinitesimal layer of surface
such that an eye could detect no difference at all.

Considering the waywardness

Considering the waywardness of all affective versions
of any account one might proffer in the face of
demands made or obligations laid down
it's no wonder the profile was laid overtop
giving one the sense that no complete or ultimate perspective
is possible in the face of impossible odds
or that lying is proliferating across the hillside
in terms of ecology what one affects to survive
or the simple fact of erosion
if there were anything one could call native to the state
all encroachment as plausible as any other.

Avoidance proper is a verb

Avoidance proper is a verb conjugated in another tongue
in routine and repetitive fashion in an Italian hilltown
in which buildings wind their bricks in circular motion
around relic fingerbones anchored in silver filigree.
To travel, not to travel, to have been traveled,
and all to be avoided in the pitiless months of rain
when women stay away from men
who stay away from the shawls and shadows they were born in.
So when she came back at the intervals she came back in
she recognized all the familiar signs,
every building slightly to the left of where it had been before.

act 3

Almost as bad, good mother,
As kill a king, and marry with his brother.

Hamlet (3.4.29–30)

No gunman waiting under the potted palm to give
me orders. I took the automatic elevator up to my
floor and walked along the hallway to the tune of
a muted radio behind a door. Something was
wrong.

RAYMOND CHANDLER, *The Big Sleep*

Act 3

It is he thinks his decision to decide when to or whether to
move in on and since then the witness has had to come to some way
of grasping his father, his mother, his uncle, his love.

Why is it the only question why really and why now and
why didn't you come with me why did you put off as I thought
all that had already gathered by Act 3 which is always

where something happens which is always my question
how does it tilt then in the direction of the ending
when nothing much more has happened yet.

The scene of the crime

A substance forming on waking coheres
as a damp scrim across a brow or under the arms
walking the hill as humidity on the underside of hills
as familiar as the one who refuses
though the argument seems one in which lines memorized
from a well-known play refuse to locate
and repeat as birds start in and before trying to focus
which seems as practiced as the day before or choreographed
for the purposes of returning to the scene of the crime
although missing the turn is as plausible as the shift
in the script is expected as on balance one always knows.

Anticipation

Anticipation stood at attention through the entire scene
what else was there to do but lean
as a dancer before lift.
Something was bound to occur.
Death in every speech and whatever he did
to hold time at bay or move it backwards
was what she also said about whether or not
she could stay the same if she didn't lift a finger
and if he'd keep on speaking there'd be no finale
and he'd hold still the April of his prime.

The missing person

Who's to say if the beautiful isn't an irritation first
an irregular bit besides.
Who's to say how fluid is wrestled to the ground.
Who's to say and never mind how much.
When her ribbon fluttered to the ground.
A missing person astride a missing cry.
Incredulity and the hillside.
Cataclysms and the final weld.

The missing memory

The crucial part is missing from the earliest light
or the excruciating sound turns out to be waking out of
one of these hotel rooms one thinks will be clearly
where it was or why one keeps trying to find
where someone has gone as flighty as before
and the outlines of the face as blurred as the birds
or why gray turns out to be morning.

That subject again

It turns out that subject again: death
and the three-headed dog
chain-smoking barflies
and all that whirled-about smoke.
Palpitations in between loss of balance
the precipice over which those who go about their business
polish shoes on their cuffs
tug a bit on their leather gloves.
All's left is the nape, one room sun-squared
and how frightening in a dress.

The remains

There's no way around it.
People will be talking.
The stone won't stay a stone
while in the room surrounded by plastic plants
they whisper what no one has seen
in the same voice he answers himself.
It was 11:30 to prove it
and the car was videotaped
for all the world to see
and the clock brought the news
replaced every so often by someone
who recalled phrases about the city
where they placed the last remains
the date when St. Francis tore off his clothes.

Bounded in a nutshell

If you can't hear the place.
If you don't know where it was put.
If you think I'm somewhere other than that.
I am certain I'm walking a cement rampart
and my hearing seems perfectly good.
Conception is the root of all evil.
It troubles my sleep though my eyes are fine.
I wake every night at four.
Well, I ask my father, is it you.
If you give a name to the place you live in.
If you recognize the one sitting across from you.
If you answer on the second ring and no one's there.

A dream itself is but a shadow

Those who show up aren't the most friendly
or garrulous or even the most potent
but there they are dreaming away in one's bed
and showing up year after year as if they expected some return.
I guess it's why they bother given how far away they live,
trying to wrest something out of a clenched-up hand.
What was the bit of polished glass or illegible smudge
and if one stares out the window to frame a thought
why the set was painted blue, why the rhythm of a wave
and why were monologues invented at all.

Mysterious rooms

Makes you think you can when you know you can't.
Makes you wish you could pry it open like a can
or lie on the line in the middle of the road
and lengthen horizons forever.

It belongs to you up close California.

It's a landscape decidedly marred.

It may have been scrawled on a billboard
but it isn't the motel room you stay in for a while
before the curtains won't leave you alone.

Acting

It's a way of making more and less of this procedure
by which it's the only way in as I see it.
Otherwise one is caught in diffusions of blond brilliance
as she leans over the parapet and either waves wildly or not
and in order to avoid the obvious hyperbole of either
elects to underhandedly or by sleight of hand
take on a manner of not exactly staying fixed
in her position or entering from the wings in a burst
of applause though one does wish to capture
the tentativeness of approach by rush and withhold,
by placing one's fingers exactly so on the keyboard.

The mother

You go not till I set you up a glass
Where you may see the inmost part of you.

Hamlet (3.4.20–21)

It's hard to know if anyone is purposefully or by intention
for reasons beyond one's ken as if seeing through doors
were as possible as walking through walls
believing it only a matter of time and in the presence of
an entire system of disbelief where it seems as if assertion
or the repetition of canticles could bring on cold sweats
and whatever follows from a given set
of what one begins to hear the longer one knows her
shrugging her shoulders, betraying her habits,
slowly closing the closet doors.

The logic of alphabets

If you think it will why won't it.
Yet it's a posture difficult to unbend.
If the room from another year is always open.
If the voice isn't closed.
If you find yourself knocking on wood.
Once is too much to forget.
We brought one to the room
filled with insect wings.
If you live as if it will.
A momentary blur out the window of a car,
a film you've seen before,
a veiled face, all profiles
and after a time everyone from the neck down.
Eyes that slant were saints
whose eyes settled it once and for all.
Everyone has the same name or it begins with A.
The name of the street you lived on once.
Your skin was thinner then.
Silk. Severity. Something something night.

Words, words, words

What was it you used to do.
What was it you said then.
Is it not the way you hear
the knock of the bird or
the intrusions of garrulous old men.
Did anyone say I don't understand
the way you talk or did anyone say
I talk the way I talk.

The reason for seduction on a maroon couch

At the beginning it seemed maroon plush
or the oddity of a warrior woven in wool
or plumage atop a column
or the behavior of a bird.
Yet the elucidation was different after all.
I hadn't originally thought the mysterious more profound
yet the guy drew my attention
and once the couch had been moved
and once the rugs rolled up
all systems were go and the fact of passion
a veritable glimpse of more than fact.

The point of no return

Can't get to the point
dangled out of reach.
How to get back from which taking off
would have located basking in the sun.
I always like to be at the shore.
Or what she assumed would make sense.
As the day grows hotter.
As each stone burns.
As the twine pulls tighter
as the kite flies higher
as the boy runs after.

A memory of the pond

If the slightly wet air in the skin is the hillside
is wherever I have to forgive what I have forgotten
is error unretrieved from clouds over ponds
is we're going swimming she said.
What I can't remember is what I can't feel—
the same moist air almost going as the cloud from hill to hill
and what she looked like when we hung about indifferent to time
    and place.
We had to forgive the backs of knees when it rained
and you can't go in during a storm she said
you can't go swimming after lunch and waiting for her to turn around
in the wet air through the length of a 40-years day.

Photographic proof

Not exactly like being followed or pried open.
Not exactly like that.
Not as if all your papers were strewn about the room
or someone had read your thoughts.
Not exactly like scratches or pores.
We all remember blithe.
We took it as a little joke.
One day arrived at the age of your mother.
And there was a photo of it or the same thing happened
as if you hadn't been through it already.
And there were children swimming
in the light of artificial strobes.
We were clammy and knew what was next.
We were all splashing.

Ophelia over the pond

Considering everything the deliberation is queasy
and the dizziness abruptly coming
and the peculiarity is foursquare upon us
and the vacancy of the vast afternoon.
It is very true what they say about the difference
between an hysteric and a saint.
It is all very well and good what they say is coming.
What is required by the very nature of the characters involved
and the tone of the situation which makes it tentative
and right then and there in a misapprehension
or the acrid smell of her wet hair.

3 why/why not

why

Explanations beside the point
a bit of fencing rather
or the grimace in the photograph of June.
She asks it over and over.
Rather the shape of the room and getting there in the dark.
If she asks why she hits her.
And a window cut in the wall.
You can see the tops of the trees burning
a bit of it hitting the electric wire.
Why should we or not move forward
and if only the place were as fixed as imposition
as forcing it on her or even asking.

By what means saying I know this or see that
or seeing it ask you to see it not so much whether it
sits on the desk or under it as prepositions or cups of tea
but how it seems to me assessing or worrying
and how like blindness it is as *under his spell*
is a form of streams running uphill.
Nearby the bridge she said she turned the wrong way
there is no bridge and in the photographs the metalwork
is as precise as the river everyone asks the name of.

I'm told you can't be in the quandary
I find myself squarely in the midst of.
But I must be where I am
whose hands I recognize in the dark
whose hair is longer this year in my hands.
I keep trying to say what I have been trying to say,
gasfumes rising in rainbows off the pavement.
No amount of explanation
and no gesture at the back of the neck.
In the picture her hair reaches to the ground
defining all that is not beautiful.

Does it matter why the bell lacks a clapper
and if not why ask when she doesn't know.
The waves in the grass from this distance
explain my standing at this distance
and the optical illusion of standing next to you.
Obfuscations are statements of love.
Everyone says is the way we say what we want
and who can say why this person walking into the room
or why translation into my heart is in my mouth.

If I want it to be what was even though I could hardly wait.
Waiting for the train in that extraordinary heat.
I found the cathedral by following bells
and what is it to wait to see you as murmurs
or glasses or proof of the benign.
One likes to say the first time one couldn't be sure.
It looked yellower than my memory
in about the middle of July how to describe
daylilies except in the mouth and under the tongue.

If I say I don't believe you is this impatience
without waiting for an answer which might take days or years.
Hard to sit still to hear what in the interstices might sing.
Again that liquid bird repeating the same story
over and over in the car as you list the placements
of adjectives and verbs out of which arises what seems
to be music in the malleable and soft folding of silver
inside an afternoon parenthesis of what was it again?

The paragraph she gives me to live in is I don't know how.
Description is a phenomenon of walks as obvious as rain.
All the outcroppings in a brownish moss I can't get over
the undulation of columns through which the distance
is an extension of how we think how someone walks.
She says you are where you should have begun.
She offers copses and seclusion,
bitterns crying in the lintels.

in someone else's shoes

Shoes are why every moment is a fact I wish I could
speak about it endlessly and one turns a phrase.
But the way it turns out takes time.
There's the being aghast or she arrives breathing hard.
Was it that woman I dreamed of then
plying streaks of cloth I never liked the idea of
or the ankles first and the arrangement of things too late to do
    much about.
The curve of the pedal nothing much to do with love.

Where we'll walk to and why and having learned
not to ask is what happened after the chunks of marble.
We wanted to weep even past the age in which such things
are what we remember what it is to rub stone
and you argue for the ecstatic without suspecting
endless ferns and endless seas.
I ruined what we can't speak about or I refuse.
The rigor of trying it out in private first.

How forward looking can we be in the midst of the future
and whose shoes should I believe everything she says
and what does it mean to stand apart or close.
She thought she was walking towards it
but how can we see it is just one moment
when she says I have to finish this conversation
and then the morning is passed and everything
is passed and speaks about it endlessly
and it turns out the building has to be hauled down bit by bit.

As a motto go slow ought to work out wondering or not
where it's going or turned out a jade green
like the underside of a gingko flipped in the sun.
Something muttered or somehow I never get to see her
meaning all the while to see her and when I am leaving
it is inevitably one of those things picked up cheap
which is like going somewhere and never leaving home.
An old postcard floats up or changing a lightbulb
in the upstairs hall who wrote the greeting from Kentucky
you try to make out the birdlike scrawl.

Why in the middle of a perfectly good season
good enough as the weatherman says blowing through
the leaving it all, not moving, crushingly so.
I name reasons as the names of nineteenth-century chairs
or list the varieties of hellebores, stained, unstained.
Malaise is a throaty sound
a pockmark, a missive, a mistimed,
the wherewithal can't do anything about, the again.

why not

OK it's over she.
No might be time.
In the midst of a cup she says will you only.
Some desires are momentary at best.
OK it's her turn.
When you cross over the line.
A lip on a cup. A cup's lip. Hers.
Hanging on for dear life or going for broke.
Her concern for the birds
her obvious concern
her birds.
It's much too sweet she says
I couldn't drink it for the life of me.

———   ———   ———

Almost immediately a chance at another.
Noon hits the patio hard.
Exotic is what she thinks does it.
Sweet tea wouldn't do it would it
never beginning with the implausible.
Oh no, not that again in the tone she uses
for dismissal and for me.
Anyhow, you might want to stake it
and put it in full sun.

When it's an obvious ploy
one's got oneself up to the neck.
A phone rings too much or not at all.
I hate finding feathers or a crow on a dead bird.
Simple natural things and the uselessness of lawns.
A divot's for bulbs you might want it.

———   ———   ———

I don't want to know you anymore.
Anyhow I don't mind it.
What is predictable all the time and the cold.
Then backing and backing and backing.
What I said was I don't mind it
and believed it when I said it.
If there's no spine
bookstores won't have it.
Those singing the blues.

Moss eats recollection.
Well if you run your hands over it.
The imagination in most is rigor in ruin.
A former life is out.
When he palmed the ace the bartender
thought he was in heaven and all the rest of us
thought so too and went out in the sun.
Why do I want to wrestle you to the ground.
Sometimes you can't even feel it but
mental exercises supposedly help.

———   ———   ———

Recall the sea then
and then recall all the other times.
If you rake the seaweed and dry it you can
burn it and the neighbors can stand around and watch.
This wasn't even yours.
Keep it afloat: slimy, dreamy, green.
Viscous is the mode of hermeneutics I'm talking about.

I'm always in the way.
Now they weigh twice as much as before.
Deft retires.
You say the way is given, a given
for those who can think.
I do see the point and retire my position
and hang up my dancing shoes.
What's a ton of feathers then.

———   ———   ———

Thistles in a sock for the birds.
Might come down and could've.
Did she say she recovered well.
What a sweet time we had even after and
what chrysanthemums we wove
the smell of them sour on the hands.
When your fingernails are green
you could be dead but you're not.

It's a covet.
Closer to a greed.
Shoved across the mantel close to the green.
The anchor was slimy with it, the chair peeling from it,
the ache was for nothing much.
Substitute a different one
see what you get.
Extend the line by arbitrary rules
take out the trash
move the inserts around your heart.

—   —   —

If love goes on and always does
what to do when it doesn't.
It's the trance behind enigma
behind wanting to have to do it.
If obligation recedes
one wants to walk in the water after it.
Have to's a primitive and maundering form.
Slip primulas in to fake it.

The object is now greener.
Transplanted from one plot to another.
In one she plays an addict and in the other
a sort of woebegone.
Her arms across her chest.
The willow in the wind.
I'd be winded also.
Imagine it drives you crazy it drives me crazy
even happening to someone else.

———   ·······   ···············

OK so you're creeping along.
Up the wall and even through it.
One tenacious case.
No interpretive data.
The sidewalk cracked and
the back of the book a case in point.
Without system, it's worthless.
It can crack you open.
Unspeakable all over the room.

The decision in absentia.
Sit cross-legged
fit to be tied
and running a fever towards noon.
Take Athens.
Take something else
and run through the pillars
with roofs on their heads.
I don't want to anymore or you
or appendages or sky.
Take Vienna
even a waltz.

—— —— ——

There's many a slip.
Up the river is a lazy song
especially at 200 yards
or a picture of it in black and white.
The band of painted sky makes a V of geese.
Then you sit and nobody says it until it's almost
a deadweight of time.
It takes until now to know it.

They all loved nature.
They all loved.
Some more than others and the green grass grows.
All windfalls ache, all what you gave me.
You take me seriously, not seriously enough, not enough.
Nature goes on, on and on they say.
Some leaves radiate along a narrow stem.
Once in a while, every once in a while.

—— —— ——

She's gotten too too.
And where would it get us to ask why.
The ramp of the incline
inclining towards uppitiness
and full of herself wouldn't be so bad
sans *infinitum* and that *fol-de-rol* of whine.
Master Thyself they say with restraint
having spent a lifetime.

No endings or beginnings or anything
that hasn't moved in on.
If everything's in relation.
If I move away or go to the other side
to the mountains where she's always wanted to be.
She's what I wanted and not now.
Sweet why have you gone so.
Clipping the hedge between one and another.

——— ——— ———   .

How can a lemon be a subject of anything
but a life gone dead or bitter over the edge.
Be still my beating heart's
another sort of matter.
Only without one is there one.
Or only without a certain sort of one.
Or only the lonely.
Every poem should have a real one.
I stuck a branch of them in a bowl and went out real quick.

Acknowledgments

Some of the poems that appear in this book were previously published in earlier versions, sometimes with different titles.

Arshile 7, 1997, "The insignificance was what," "Avoidance proper is a verb," "In the church with angel heads," "Unable to keep the spill from spilling," "The decisions are already past the time," "If it is someone else's rent"

The Chicago Review 24, no. 1, 1999, "The object is now greener"

Denver Quarterly 36, no. 1/2, 2001, "Anticipation," "*Bounded in a nutshell*," "Acting," "The Mother #1," "*Words, Words, Words*," "Ophelia over the pond," "The scene of the crime"

Field 65, fall 2001, "The logic of alphabets"

Inscape 1, spring 1998, "Photographic proof," "The missing person"

Inscape 3, fall 1999, "It's a covet," "The object is now greener," "Ok so you're creeping along"

Interim 17, no. 2, 1998, "And so geography," "The paragraph she gives me to live in"

Jubilat 2, 2000, "Explanations beside the point"

lipstick eleven, no. 2, 2001, Selections from "Why not"

New American Writing 19, 2001, "Those who show up"

Quotidian, a+bend chapbook, 2000, "In the perplexities," "Each had been reading," "Sitting with my feet to the side," "It might have been his usual demeanor," "After the dark came," "Your feet on the same steps"

Rhizome 3, 1999, "When it's an obvious ploy," "I'm always in the way," "I don't want to know you anymore," "Almost immediately," "Moss eats recollection"

Ribot 4, 1996, "How often, meaning," "Hopelessly lost"

The Southern Review 35, spring 1999, Odi et amo poems: "Why is the cure for irony," "Do you think so," "Allegory is the only way to conclusion"

The Southern Review 38, spring 2002, "Why knowing is," "That subject again"

26: A Journal of Poetry and Poetics, issue A, 2002, "At odds with defeats love," "Why is as why does," "Does it matter why the bell," "How forward looking can we be," "As a motto go slow ought to work"

Design	*Victoria Kuskowski*
Compositor	*BookMatters, Berkeley*
Text	*10.25/15 Filosofia Regular*
Display	*Garamond Antiqua*
Printer and binder	*Friesens Corporation*